People in a Family

Katie Peters

GRL Consultant Diane Craig,
Certified Literacy Specialist

Pull Ahead READERS

Lerner Publications ◆ Minneapolis

Note from a GRL Consultant
This Pull Ahead leveled book has been carefully designed for beginning readers. A team of guided reading literacy experts has reviewed and leveled the book to ensure readers pull ahead and experience success.

Lerner Publications
An imprint of Lerner Publishing Group, Inc.
241 First Avenue North
Minneapolis, MN 55401 USA

For reading levels and more information, look up this title at www.lernerbooks.com.

Main body text set in Memphis Pro 24/39
Typeface provided by Linotype.

Photo Acknowledgments
The images in this book are used with the permission of: © Pixel-Shot/Shutterstock, pp. 3; © Miljan Zivkovic/Shutterstock, pp. 4–5; © Fernanda_Reyes/Shutterstock, pp. 6–7, 16 (left); © Diego Cervo/Shutterstock, pp. 8–9, 16 (right); © fizkes/Shutterstock, pp. 10–11, 16 (middle); © Prostock-studio/Shutterstock, pp. 12–13; © Rido/Shutterstock, pp. 14–15.

Front cover: © PeopleImages.com - Yuri A/Shutterstock

Library of Congress Cataloging-in-Publication Data

Names: Peters, Katie author
Title: People in a family / written by Katie Peters.
Description: Minneapolis : Lerner Publications, [2026] | Series: Let's look at families | Includes index. | Audience: Ages 4–7 | Audience: Grades K–1 | Summary: "Some families have a mom and a dad; some have a grandma and grandpa. Engaging photographs and text help readers explore all kinds of families. Pairs with the fiction story, Who's in Ada's Family?"—Provided by publisher.
Identifiers: LCCN 2025011174 (print) | LCCN 2025011175 (ebook) | ISBN 9798765689837 library binding | ISBN 9798348028558 paperback | ISBN 9798765694985 epub
Subjects: LCSH: Families—Juvenile literature
Classification: LCC HQ744 .P395 2026 (print) | LCC HQ744 (ebook) | DDC 306.85—dc23/eng/20250512

LC record available at https://lccn.loc.gov/2025011174
LC ebook record available at https://lccn.loc.gov/2025011175

Manufactured in the United States of America
1 – CG – 12/15/25

Table of Contents

People in a Family

This is my dad.

This is my sister.

This is my grandpa.

This is my uncle.

This is my mom.

This is my family.

Did You See It?

backpack

dinosaur

guitar

Index